# CONTENTS

Published by Smart Apple Media,
an imprint of Black Rabbit Books
P.O. Box 3263, Mankato, Minnesota 56002
www.blackrabbitbooks.com

Published by arrangement with
The Salariya Book Company Ltd

Cataloging-in-Publication Data is available
from the Library of Congress

Printed in the United States
At Corporate Graphics,
North Mankato, Minnesota

9 8 7 6 5 4 3 2 1

ISBN: 978-1-62588-357-5

Photographic credits
t=top b=bottom c=center l=left r=right

The Art Archive/ Belvoir Castle/ Eileen Tweedy: 34/35t
The Art Archive/ Eileen Tweedy: 18/19, 34b
The Art Archive/ JFB: 17r
The Art Archive/ Harper Collins Publishers: 30
The Art Archive/ Musée des Beaux Art Nantes/ Dagli Orti: 20 bl
The Art Archive/ Musée du Château de Versailles/ Dagli Orti: 28bl
The Art Archive/ National Archives Washington DC: 38t-, 39c
The Art Archive/ Wellington Museum, London/ Eileen Tweedy: 31tl
Ashmolean Museum, Oxford, UK/ The Bridgeman Art Library: 15br
Breslich and Foss: 22r, 23l, 33l, 36l, 37r, 41l
Bridgeman Art Library: 12/13, 25tl
Cheltenham Art Gallery and Museum, Gloucestershire, UK/ The Giraudon/ The Bridgeman Art Library: 25tr
Kunsthistorisches Museum, Vienna, Austria/ The Bridgeman Art Library: 10tl
Mountain High Maps/ copyright 1993 Digital Wisdom Inc: 6/7c, 8tl, 10r, 12tl, 13tl, 16tl, 18tr, 20tl, 22tr, 26tl, 30tr, 36tl
Nigel Hillyard of The Sealed Knot: 14l, 15tl
Smith Art Gallery and Museum, Stirling, Scotland/ The Bridgeman Art Library: 19tr
Victoria and Albert Museum, London, UK/ The Bridgeman Art Library: 21tl

©The Salariya Book Company: 1, 2/3, 5, 9, 11br, 13t, 19:l, 22bc, 27tr, 27l, 29r, 31tr, 31r, 35bl, 37cl, 37b, 40tr, 41bl, 46/47, 48

Every effort has been made to trace copyright holders. The Salariya Book Company apologises for any unintentional omissions and would be pleased, in such cases, to add an acknowledgement in future editions.

# Warriors III

## Warfare in the 16th to 19th Century

### in the 16th to 19th Century

Written and illustrated by
**Mark Bergin**

A+
**Smart Apple Media**

# OVERVIEW

**B**etween the 16<sup>th</sup> and 19<sup>th</sup> centuries many conflicts were fought around the globe. These were partly due to the ideologies and expansionist policies of countries and their rulers. Over this period, military strategies and fighting techniques changed dramatically with the use of new weapons, such as gunpowder. By mobilizing strong armies and navies to control more of the world's surface, European powers planned to build vast empires in the 16<sup>th</sup> and 17<sup>th</sup> centuries. Many of the wars in the following period saw those empires crumble as occupied territories tried to fight back.

ARMADA, 1588
In 1588, King Philip II of Spain sent a large invasion fleet to attack Elizabeth I's England. This was successfully fought off by a smaller fleet led by Sir Francis Drake.

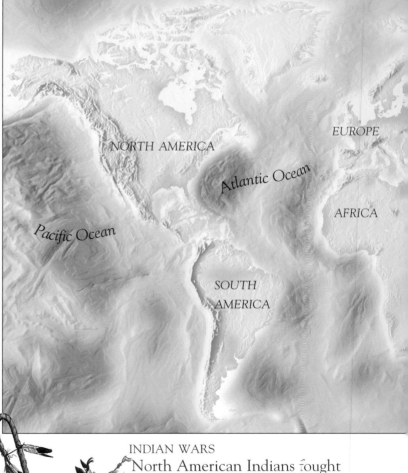

NORTH AMERICA

EUROPE

*Atlantic Ocean*

AFRICA

*Pacific Ocean*

SOUTH AMERICA

REVOLUTIONARY WAR
Although Britain's armed forces were among the best in the world, the American colonies rebelled against them in 1775 to claim their freedom. They were helped by Britain's old enemies, the French and Spanish.

U.S. CIVIL WAR
The American Civil War (1861–1865) was one of the most significant events in the history of the United States. Three million soldiers fought on both sides in the conflict. Northern (Union) states and southern (Confederate) states fought each other over whether the national government or the individual states should have more power.

INDIAN WARS
North American Indians fought many battles with the new settlers who colonized their land. The new settlers brought diseases, put up boundaries on native hunting grounds, and slaughtered buffalo herds. By the 1860s, the U.S. government moved many tribes to reservations, but many chose to fight against such oppression.

### ENGLISH CIVIL WAR
King Charles I and Parliament fought over the power to govern the country between 1642 and 1643. The country was divided in its support for either side.

### JACOBITE REBELLION
In 1745, an uprising was led in Scotland by Prince Charles Stuart. He sailed from France and united various clan leaders to take the crown of England from King George II.

### FREDERICK THE GREAT
Frederick (ruled 1740-1786) was king of Prussia (present-day northern Germany). He increased Prussia's territory and influence by campaigning against his neighbors in the Seven Years' War.

RUSSIA

JAPAN

### CRIMEAN WAR
The Crimean War was caused by a dispute between Russia, France, and the Ottoman Empire. They fought over the rights of protection of Christian shrines in the Ottoman-controlled holy land.

### SAMURAI WARLORDS
The samurai were the military elite of Japan, similar to the medieval knights of Europe. Their military power and political skills enabled them to control local governments and lands. Samurai clans were in a continual state of civil war until 1603, when they all came under the ruling dynasty of Tokugawa Ieyasu.

### NAPOLEONIC WARS
Napoleon was one of the greatest commanders in history. He changed the borders in Europe between 1799 and 1815. This French general had ambitious plans to conquer all of Europe and then Russia as well. This led to a 15-year period of turmoil and battles around Europe, from Spain to Russia.

Japan

*Mounted samurai warriors ride out from Himeji Castle (below)*

## SAMURAI CASTLES

Samurai castles were situated to guard the routes connecting the *daimyo* (warlord) territories with hostile neighboring lands. If a site lacked strong natural defenses, artificial barriers, such as moats and walls, were built. Between 1570 and 1690, the golden age of Japanese castle construction occurred.

# SHOGUNS AND SAMURAI

The samurai were the warrior class who served local lords in medieval Japan. Military families had dominated Japan from around the 12$^{th}$ century, after the emperor had been replaced by a military overlord, called a *shogun*. Many years of turmoil followed, with continual outbreaks of fighting between rival lords. Throughout these years of unrest, the samurai followed the code of *bushido* (the way of the warrior). The basis of this code was an unquestioning loyalty to one's lord. This bond of service was often so strong that if a lord died in battle, his followers might commit mass suicide rather than surrender or serve another lord.

The Battle of Sekigahara, on October 21$^{st}$, 1600, was the most decisive in the history of Japan. Ishida Mitsunari (with 100,000 troops) and Tokugawa Ieyasu (with 75,000 troops) fought to be master of Japan. After a fierce hand-to-hand battle, 30,000 men lay dead. Ieyasu won and was given the title of Shogun three years later.

## HIMEJI CASTLE

The castle (above and below) was completed in 1609. This beautiful structure was covered in intricately carved and painted woodwork. Other features included multiple gateways, courtyards, reception halls, watchtowers, stables, and workshops.

**TYPES OF SAMURAI WARRIORS**

a. An archer's "kyudo" bamboo bow could be shot from horseback or standing.

b. An *arquebusier* was a samurai with a type of musket.

c. A spearman carried spears up to 5 yards long.

d. A standard-bearer.

e. An army commander wore full metal armor and a *kabuto* (crested helmet).

f. Bodyguard with a *daito* (long sword).

g. Low-class *bushi* (foot soldier) armed with a *nagamaki* (a kind of slashing spear with a long wooden handle and a sword-like blade).

**ARMOR**

Elaborate samurai armor (below) was made from lacquered iron and leather segments held together with silk cords. The sleeves and legs were made from chain mail, and helmets often had crests and iron face masks. Attached to their backs were colorful banners with their clan's crests on them.

*Head detail from a samurai suit of armor*

# ARMADA, 1588

*A 16th-century portrait of Sir Francis Drake*

Sir Francis Drake (above) was one of the most feared captains at sea. He had sailed around the world in his ship the *Golden Hinde* (1577–1580) looking for treasure. In 1587, Drake led a force of 25 ships and made a series of devastating attacks against Spanish ports.

Philip II of Spain had plenty of reasons to go to war with England. English privateers were raiding Spanish ports and ships, and Queen Elizabeth I's government was persecuting Catholics in England. Philip's plan was for two forces to link up, cross the channel, and attack—from Spain the Duke of Medina Sidonia's fleet, and from the Spanish Netherlands the Duke of Parma's army. The Armada of 130 ships and 19,000 troops set sail on May 28th, 1588, from Lisbon. After some minor skirmishes at sea, the Spanish anchored off Calais and were attacked at night by English fireships. Scattered, the Armada was considerably damaged in a nine-hour battle between Gravelines (France) and Ostend (in what is now Belgium). A strong south-westerly wind drove the remaining ships into the North Sea, and Spanish commanders ordered them to return home by routing north of Scotland and the Irish Sea.

*Map showing the route taken by the Spanish Armada (right)*

In the initial battles with the Armada, the English were so far out of range that their cannon did little damage. But after the Battle of Plymouth, the Spanish ship *San Salvador* blew up, and the *Rosario* was captured by Drake after losing a mast.

*Drake looks at the Spanish fleet from the deck of an English galleon (left)*

_Ark Royal_

### ARK ROYAL

English ships fought at long range with their guns, whereas the Spanish ships were designed to fight traditionally, closing in on and boarding with masses of soldiers. The English flagship was the _Ark Royal_ (left), built in 1587. The gun ports were placed below decks but well above the water-line. The ship had 24 gunners, 150 sailors, and 76 soldiers on board.

### SPANISH SHIPS

The Armada flagship was the Portuguese galleon _San Martin_ (below), with 48 guns. Other

Armada ships were galleasses (with sails and oars) and galleys (with oars only). Galleasses were slow but heavily armed. Just after the Armada set sail, rough seas forced the fleet's four galleys to turn back.

_Spanish ship wrecked by storms_

### THE WEATHER TAKES ITS TOLL

Storms lashed the Armada on its route around Scotland and Ireland. Many ships were lost along the coast, forced ashore and smashed on the rocks (above). The leader of the Armada, Medina Sidonia, got his flagship back to Spain on September 21st. Around 15,000 men never returned, and less than half the ships made it into port.

_A "morion" helmet as worn by Spanish soldiers in the Armada_

# ENGLISH CIVIL WAR

onflict arose between Charles I of England and Parliament over how to deal with Scotland and Ireland. The king was causing religious unrest in both of these countries by enforcing Protestant rule. Charles needed money from taxes to do this, but Parliament refused to help him. They demanded that he dismiss some of his senior aides, whom they distrusted. When Charles attempted to arrest five troublesome members of Parliament on January 4th, 1642, he angered many people and riots broke out in London. The king was forced to flee the city. By October, the king had raised an army of 13,000 men, and they headed toward London. Under the leadership of the earl of Essex, the Parliamentary troops left the capital to cut him off. The forces first met at Edgehill (October 23rd). The king narrowly won this battle but later retreated to establish headquarters in Oxford. Although the Royalists had success in much of England, especially in the southwest (capturing Bristol on July 26th, 1643), Charles still did not advance on London.

*A "mortuary hilt" sword, as used by cavalry soldiers during the Civil War*

## MAJOR BATTLES

The map above shows the principal battles between the Royalists (Cavaliers) and the Parliamentarians (Roundheads).

*A 19th-century painting of the Battle of Marston Moor, 1644 (below)*

## MARSTON MOOR, JULY 2ND, 1644

Under Leslie, first earl of Leven, the Scots came south and joined with the Parliamentary forces. At the Battle of Marston Moor (below), near York, these forces crushed the Royalists, led by Prince Rupert (the king's nephew and duke of Newcastle). York now surrendered to the Parliamentarian army and the Scots stormed Newcastle on October 19th, with 21,000 men.

# NEW MODEL ARMY

In the winter of 1644–1645, the British Parliament suffered heavy defeats and was having problems with its army regarding salary disputes. The solution was to bring together old army units under the leadership of commanders Sir Thomas Fairfax and Oliver Cromwell. This was known as the "New Model Army," consisting of 22,000 full-time paid and trained men. This army met and defeated the Royalists at Naseby on June 14th, 1645, and by May of 1646, the king was under siege at Oxford. The Civil War officially ended when Oxford surrendered to Parliament on June 24th, but the king escaped from the city in disguise and gave himself up to the Scots. At first, the Scots would not help Charles, because he would not agree to their demands. Having again escaped Cromwell's clutches, Charles eventually persuaded the Scots to help him, but their army was defeated by Cromwell and Fairfax at the Battle of Preston in 1648. The king was taken under arrest to Windsor, and after a vote in Parliament, King Charles was made to stand trial as a traitor to his country. He was sentenced to death and executed by having his head cut off.

## ARTILLERY

The heavy artillery of an army was stationed at the rear, where it could fire over the heads of the infantry.

*Reconstruction of a small cannon used in the English Civil War*

Smaller cannons (left), that fired nails and scrap iron in canvas bags, were positioned in front of the infantry.

*Helmet*

*Leather tunic*

*Short-barreled musket*

*Roundheads wore red sashes early in the war to identify themselves in battle*

## CAVALRYMEN

These soldiers carried a sword and a short-barreled musket. The main strategy was to advance at a quick trot until in range of the enemy. The men in the front fired, then wheeled away. In their second charge, they advanced at a gallop using their swords.

THE DEATH OF A KING
After a week-long trial, King Charles I was executed on January 30th, 1649 (above). Before his head was cut off, his final words were, "I am a martyr to the people." Oliver Cromwell had signed the King's death warrant himself.

*Reconstruction of pikemen from the English Civil War*

### PIKEMEN
Pikemen (above) were foot soldiers armed with 16-foot-long pointed pikes. They stood at the center of battle formations to keep advancing enemy cavalry at bay. Well-disciplined pikemen, brave enough to hold their ground, could do tremendous damage to cavalry charging straight at them.

*Death mask of Oliver Cromwell (right), made by taking a wax impression of his face at the time of his death*

### TYRANT OR SAVIOR?
After the execution of Charles I, Oliver Cromwell brutally suppressed uprisings in both Scotland and Ireland. A new Parliament was formed, consisting of 140 "godly" (religious) men who made Cromwell "Lord Protector" (temporary Head of State). His first act was to make a peace treaty with the Dutch in 1654, which ended years of trade wars and helped the British Empire expand overseas.

# War of the Spanish Succession, 1701–1714

At the end of the 17th century, the king of Spain, Charles II, died without an heir. All of Europe fought for the vast territories owned by the Hapsburg family, which included large parts of Europe and lands in the Americas. It soon became a struggle between the two most powerful families in Europe, the Hapsburgs under Leopold I and the Bourbons under Louis XIV. Fearing that one nation might become too powerful, the British and their Dutch allies sided with Leopold I to stop the French from becoming a European superpower.

**JOHN CHURCHILL, DUKE OF MARLBOROUGH**
During the war, English commander Marlborough (right) waged ten successful campaigns, besieged over thirty towns, and never lost a battle or contest.

Duke of Marlborough

**CHAIN OF COMMAND**
Marlborough's army was well organized. He relayed messages through "aides-de-camp" (below), foot-runners who acted as his eyes and ears on the battlefield.

Aide-de-camp

Long coat

Sword

In 1702, the duke of Marlborough joined forces with Prince Eugene of Savoy to prevent the French from advancing on Vienna, Austria. The armies fought near the German village of Blenheim in August 1704, where the French and German forces lost around 30,000 men. Later in the war, in 1708, Marlborough scored a decisive victory over the French duke of Vendome at the battle of Oudenarde. Following this victory, the war was brought to a conclusion as the British and Dutch forces overwhelmed their enemies over the next few years.

The French army of Louis XIV (above) had long coats, waistcoats, pants, and stockings. Each carried a sword and flintlock musket with a bayonet. Sergeants wore cuffs edged with gold lace.

**DRAGONS**
DE MONSEIGNEUR LE DUC
**DE PENTHIEVRE,**
En Garnison à Quimper, en Bretagné.

PROPAGANDA
Recruiting poster (above) for the dragoons of the duke of Vendome, who was also known as the duke of Penthievre. Dragoons were heavily armed mounted military troops.

Flintlock musket with bayonet

Cannon

Drum

# JACOBITE REBELLION

Great Britain

In 1708, the unpopular English king, James II, had been replaced on the throne by his daughter, Mary, and her husband, William. After a failed uprising in 1715, James fled to France. A generation later, the Jacobites (supporters of James) were led by his grandson, Charles Stuart, also known as "Bonnie Prince Charlie." Charles hoped to get support from France, which was at war with England. A small invasion force set sail from France in July 1745, but it was intercepted by the Royal Navy. The Prince's ship escaped. He landed in Scotland and began to drum up support from the Highland clans. With their help, they had captured Edinburgh with 2,500 men by September.

Charles's force marched over the border into England and took control of Carlisle after a six-day siege. The force now advanced towards London but, discouraged by lack of French support, the highland chiefs forced Charles to turn back on December 6th. The final battle of the uprising was at Culloden on April 16th, 1746. A larger British force, under the command of the duke of Cumberland, dealt a decisive blow and shattered the rebel army.

Duke of Cumberland

CULLODEN
As Charles deserted the battlefield at Culloden, Cumberland (right) ordered his soldiers to show no mercy to the highlanders. They were slaughtered in retreat, and Cumberland became known as "the Butcher."

## HIGHLANDER'S SWORD

The basket-hilt broadsword (left) would have been used at Culloden. The full sword is several feet long. The hilt was designed to encase the user's hand, protecting it from enemy blows.

## BONNIE PRINCE CHARLIE

Charles Stuart (above) was 25 years old at the time of the rebellion. He escaped and married in 1772 but had no children. He was the last Stuart to fight for the British throne.

*Mitre-style hat*

*Musket*

*Match case*

## GRENADIER

On the left is a typical English soldier of the 1745 period. The royal crown and white horse of Hanover is seen on his mitre-style hat. He has two pouches: one for grenades, and one for carrying cartridges. He also has a brass match case fixed above the buckle to store matches for lighting the grenades. He wears long marching gaiters.

*Marching gaiters*

# FREDERICK THE GREAT

Frederick the Great of Prussia (part of modern Germany and Poland) had a well-trained army. He used it to great effect when he invaded the Austrian-ruled land of Silesia (part of present-day Poland) on December 16th, 1740. The Austrians, weakened by a recent war with the Ottomans, were not expecting the attack, and so the province quickly fell.

In 1741, Frederick invaded Bohemia (in the present-day Czech Republic), capturing Prague after a short siege.

In 1745, the Austrians, under Charles of Lorraine, were determined to drive the Prussians from Silesia but were out-maneuvered by Frederick's well-drilled infantry and cavalry. These victories forced the Austrians to accept the Prussian claim to Silesia at the Peace of Dresden. Due to the rise of Prussia, Russia and Austria allied themselves to crush their expanding enemy. Between 1756 and 1763, most of Europe was at war. France sided with Russia and Austria, while Britain, Sweden, and Germany allied themselves with Prussia. Finally, in 1762, a Russo-Prussian peace was ordered by Peter III of Russia, and hostilities ceased. The Austrians followed suit on February 15th, 1763.

*Musket with bayonet*

## A GREAT LEADER

Frederick II (left) spent his childhood in rigorous military training and education. As an adult, he studied music and French literature. He directed the internal affairs of his country with passion and prudence. By the time he died, he had nearly doubled the area of the Prussian kingdom.

## PRUSSIAN INFANTRY

Frederick the Great's army was well-paid and well-equipped. It had grown to 154,000 men by 1756. His army was adept at drills and discipline, and in time could move into position flawlessly to execute complex tactics. The Prussian infantry carried flintlock muskets with bayonets.

*Marching gaiters*

This image (left) depicts soldiers in red, yellow and white uniforms. It is from a 1789 publication entitled *Preussische Armee Uniformen unter Friedrich Wilhelm II*, meaning "Prussian Army Uniforms under Frederick William II."

*Frederick the Great*

A BRAVE LEADER

Twice, Frederick was wounded on the battlefield when the horse he was riding was shot. He is pictured below with two of the 5th Hussars (a unit of light cavalry soldiers).

*Hussar*

# AMERICAN REVOLUTION, 1775–1783

America

Recreation of a British soldier

Felt hat

Bayonet

*A*fter a series of expensive conflicts in Europe, Britain decided to raise money by increasing the taxes of its American colonists. The people of the thirteen colonies in America were deeply unhappy about paying these taxes. They didn't think it was fair because they had no representation in the English Parliament.

When the British attempted to seize a large arms supply at Concord in Massachusetts, the Americans fought back. Although the casualties were relatively low, the war and the fight for freedom had begun.

REDCOATS
This British soldier (right) is in full marching uniform, with a knapsack, felt hat, and gaiters. He also carries a flintlock rifle with a removable bayonet.

A "lion's head" saber, as used by naval officers

Flintlock rifle

THE WAR AT SEA
American privateers caused problems for British trade ships but did not threaten the British Navy until the French entered the war in 1778. After this, there were many battles in the waters off America (above).

Gaiters

## CONTINENTALS

In 1776, George Washington persuaded Congress to raise a Continental regular army. Each state provided soldiers for the force. The soldiers were given a musket, cartridge box, bayonet belt, and coat. They had to supply their own shirts, breeches, socks, and shoes.

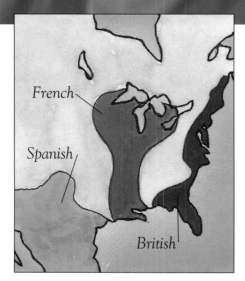

*Map of the east side of North America (above), showing how the land was divided among the colonial powers before the Seven Years' War*

Musket

Bayonet

Breeches

*Recreation of a soldier in Washington's Continental army*

## THE SEVEN YEARS' WAR

Europe had been in turmoil between 1756 and 1763, with Britain and Prussia fighting against France and Austria because of commercial and colonial rivalry (see pages 20–21). There were bitter disputes between Britain and France over territory in North America, and this led the French to join the campaign to rid the continent of British rule.

## MINUTEMEN

Each American colony had a group of volunteer soldiers called "minutemen" (below left). They were expected to be ready to fight at a minute's notice. These soldiers had the words "Liberty or Death" on their caps and carried their belongings wrapped in a blanket worn as a bandolier, which helped them carry ammunition.

Minuteman

Continental soldiers

Bandolier

# BATTLES FOR INDEPENDENCE

*I*n the Autumn of 1775, the Americans invaded Canada in an attempt to cut off the British soldiers in New England. After a six-week siege, Fort St. Jean surrendered, as did the forces at Fort Chambly and Montreal. In 1777, the British tried to cut the thirteen colonies in half. They won victories at Brandywine and Germantown, but the strategy failed after battles at Bemis Heights and Bennington. With the arrival of the French in 1778, the power balance shifted, and the British moved south. The end of the war came with the Battle of Yorktown, Virginia, in 1781 (below). The British force, under General Cornwallis, was surrounded by the forces of Washington (American) and Rochambeau (French). America had finally won its independence.

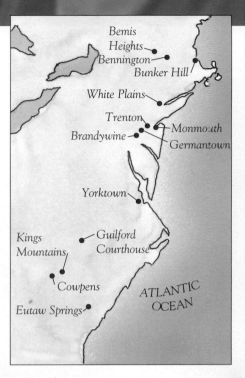

*Map (above) showing the major battles of the American War of Independence, from Bunker Hill to the British surrender at Yorktown in 1781*

*An 18th-century oil painting depicting British troops attacking the Americans at the Battle of Bunker Hill*

*An 18th-century colored engraving depicting the British surrendering to George Washington after their defeat at Yorktown*

BUNKER HILL, JUNE 17TH, 1775

The first major battle of the war took place at Bunker Hill (above). The Americans, who were entrenched on top of the hill, inflicted heavy casualties on the British lines of infantry. However, when the Americans ran out of ammunition, the British eventually drove them back.

BRITISH SURRENDER

Besieged at Yorktown, Cornwallis and the British troops sustained heavy bombardment for 14 days. British ships bringing more troops to relieve Yorktown were blocked at Virginia Capes by the French Navy under Admiral De Grasse. Under constant fire and with no sign of relief, Cornwallis surrendered (above).

*Continentals bombarding Yorktown with artillery*

# NAPOLEONIC WARS, 1797–1815

Europe and North Africa

Napoleon Bonaparte

Napoleon rose out of the chaos of the violent revolution in France (1787–1799), in which the king, queen, and thousands of others were executed. Born in Corsica in 1769, the young Napoleon was sent to French military school and graduated to become a lieutenant in the artillery. By 1796, he had taken command of the French army in Italy to counter the threat of an Austrian invasion. Within a year, he had driven them out. He fought with new tactics, often marching at night, attacking in the rain, and even fighting on Sundays, which had been unheard of before. Napoleon next attacked Egypt to disrupt the British trade routes there. At first he was successful. He won the Battle of Cairo on July 21st, 1798, and defeated the Egyptian Mamelukes army at Giza, capturing Suez. However, at the Battle of the Nile on August 1st, 1798, the French fleet was destroyed. They lost six ships (four sunk, two captured) to British Admiral Nelson.

Bearskin helmet

Cartridge box

Flintlock musket

*Recreation of soldiers from the Napoleonic Imperial Guard*

## SHAKO PLATE

Worn on the front of a soldier's helmet, the shako plate (above) was decorated with the symbol of an eagle and marked with the maxim of the French Republic: "Liberté, Egalité, Fraternité" (Freedom, Equality, Brotherhood).

Hussar

Polish Lancer

Dragoon

## UNIFORMS

The Napoleonic era was a "golden age" of military uniforms (above and right), which were as grand as possible, both to impress the enemy and to raise the morale of the wearer. Unfortunately, these fancy uniforms were usually impractical.

# NELSON'S NAVY

It has been said that all that separated Britain from an invasion by Napoleon were the ships of the British Navy (nicknamed the "Wooden Walls").
In 1789, there were around 16,000 officers and men in naval service. By 1803, this number had risen to 120,000 because of the war with France. At this time, the Navy had over 110 warships that were used to defend the country, attack enemy navies, control distant colonies, and protect merchant ships. Britain's strong sea power made the country one of the most powerful nations in the world during this period.

## NELSON (1758–1805)
Horatio Nelson rose rapidly through the ranks to become a captain at the age of 21. His bold leadership brought him decisive victories at the Nile (1798) and Copenhagen (1801). His most famous victory at the Battle of Trafalgar (1805) cost him his life.

## MEMBERS OF THE CREW
The crew of a ship like the *Victory* was enormous: 600 strong, including 150 marines, as well as 20 officers, lieutenants, and the captain.

*Captain*

*Lieutenant*

*Midshipman (with a speaking trumpet)*

*"Powder monkey" – a man who supplied the gunners with gunpowder*

*Horatio Nelson*

Gun crews (above) worked quickly on deck. It took an experienced crew two to five minutes to clean, load, aim, and fire a cannon.

## VARIOUS AMMUNITION
There were different types of projectiles used for different purposes, such as to cut down sails and rigging, to kill enemy soldiers, and to penetrate the wooden hulls of enemy ships.

*Various types of ammunition*

## HMS VICTORY

Nelson's flagship, the *HMS Victory* (below), was built between 1759–1765 using 2,000 oak trees. The *Victory* was a "first rate" ship, meaning it had over 100 cannons. These were distributed along four gun decks on each side of the ship.

*HMS Victory*

*Detail from the HMS Victory*

Gun ports

Large ships like the Victory were difficult to handle. It had 32 different sails and about 24 miles of rigging.

## CROSSING THE LINE

Tactics were to "cross the line" (right) of enemy fleets to separate them into smaller units and enable all guns to fire at once on a target.

*Diagram showing how a ship would "cross the line"*

## BATTLE OF TRAFALGAR, 1805

In 1805, Napoleon planned to invade Britain. He ordered Admiral Villeneuve's combined Franco-Spanish fleet to make a diversionary voyage, before returning to cover the invasion. Nelson chased  this fleet back to Spain and the invasion plan was abandoned. The Franco-Spanish fleet then sailed to support French forces in the Mediterranean. Nelson's fleet of 27 ships intercepted it at Cape Trafalgar (off the Spanish coast) on October 21$^{st}$ and after an epic sea battle (above), 19 of Napoleon's 33 ships surrendered or were destroyed.

# PENINSULAR WARS

In 1804, Napoleon appointed himself emperor of France. In the following years he had great military successes, first against the Russians and Austrians at Austerlitz and later against the Prussians in a series of lightning attacks. In 1807, Napoleon enforced a blockade of British trade. He did this by invading Spain and Portugal, where he installed his cousin, Joseph Bonaparte, as king. British General Sir Arthur Wellesly landed a small army in Portugal to drive the French out and the Peninsular Wars began. Although Wellesly won initial battles at Rolica and Vimiero, the British were forced to retreat to Corunna for the winter. Wellesly then advanced rapidly and drove the French out of Portugal. In 1810, the French, under Marshal Massena, invaded Spain and Portugal once more but were defeated at Fuentes d'Onoro (1811) and Salamanca (1812). After five years of bloody conflict, the Peninsular Wars ended in 1813, when the French evacuated Madrid. It signalled an end to the French domination of Europe.

Map showing the Spanish peninsula and the major battles of the campaign

THE BATTLE OF SALAMANCA
This was a decisive blow to Napoleon's grip on the Spanish peninsula. More than 7,000 French troops were killed, and a further 7,000 were captured, when they tried to attack the Duke of Wellington's army near Salamanca (below).

Captured French troops being led into Salamanca (below)

*A flintlock pistol from the Napoleonic era*

As well as a saber, French cavalry troops would have carried a pistol (above)

Peaked helmet

Curved sword

Decorative tassels in the hussar style

ARTHUR WELLESLY, DUKE OF WELLINGTON

Known as "The Iron Duke" by his soldiers, Wellesly (above) was born in Ireland and joined the British army in 1787. In 1796, he was sent to India and became a prominent soldier and administrator. On his return to Britain, he was knighted. He took command of the British forces against Napoleon in the Peninsular Wars and was made duke of Wellington in 1814.

CAVALRY

Troops on horseback were divided into heavy and light units. Heavy cavalry were used for shock tactics and would try to smash through the enemy line by brute force. The light cavalry (right), used mostly for flanking maneuvers and pursuit, wore no armor and carried curved swords for slashing. Massed for the attack, they were an imposing sight. Walking slowly towards the enemy's troops, they patiently waited for the signal to charge as gun shot and shell rained down on them.

*Recreation of a member of the British light dragoons*

# ROAD TO WATERLOO

In 1813, Austria and Prussia rose up to fight the French. While Napoleon defended his territory in Germany, Wellington advanced through Spain and entered France from the south in the spring of 1814. While Napoleon tried to resist an invasion from the eastern allies, he was unable to stop Paris from falling to an allied coalition. He was forced to give up the throne and go into exile on the island of Elba. However,

in March 1815, he escaped and returned to France, where he still had the support of his old guard. On June 16th, he made a sudden advance into Belgium and defeated the Prussian General Blucher at the Battle of Ligny. Napoleon's final stand was on June 18th, when he met Wellington's army at Waterloo in Belgium. With Prussian help, Wellington defeated Napoleon, and the once-great military commander went into exile for good on the island of St Helena.

FIRING A BROWN BESS FLINTLOCK

a. Take a cartridge from side pouch and bite off the end.
b. Pour a small amount of powder on the priming pan.
c. Put the ball and paper down the muzzle of the musket.
d. Use the ramrod to push the ball down to the end of the barrel.
e. Pull the cock back with thumb. This has the striking flint in it.
f. Take aim.
g. Fire!

THE BROWN BESS FLINTLOCK
This smoothbore, muzzle-loading, flintlock musket was used by British troops in the Napoleonic Wars. Well-trained infantry could fire three rounds per minute, an incredible rate considering the number of stages required to load the weapon. Although the musket's effective range was roughly 150 yards, British troops normally held their fire until the enemy were as close as 60 yards. At this distance a volley of fire would be deadly.

*Brown Bess flintlock musket*

## BRITISH INFANTRY REDCOAT

Most young men joined the army for the money and few for adventure and glory. They weren't paid particularly well—a shilling (12¢) a day, of which a majority was kept for expenses—but if you were a penniless laborer this was much better than starving.

*Recreation of a British infantry redcoat from the Napoleonic era*

Blanket

Musket

Ration bag

Cartridge box

## BRITISH BATTLE FORMATIONS

The "square" was the best formation for defense against cavalry attack. Soldiers would line up on each side of a square in four ranks. This meant that two ranks could fire while two were reloading. The officers and the company flags were in the center. Another tactic, the "thin red line," consisted of two ranks of infantry used to fire at three sides of an attacking column of French infantry.

The "thin red line"

Infantry

Enemy infantry

The "square"

Infantry ranks

Officers and flags

# CRIMEAN WAR, 1854–1856

When Russia marched into Ottoman territories across the River Danube in March 1854, both Britain and France were concerned. Britain was fearful that Russia would threaten British trade with India. The new leader of France, Napoleon III, was worried about French interests in that area. So, on March 28th, 1854, Britain and France declared war on Russia. The allied forces, led by Lord Ragland (British) and Marshal St. Arnaud (French), reached the Black Sea in August, 1854. On September 14th, the allies landed at Eupatoria on the Crimean coast. The inferior Russian forces were defeated at the Alma River on September 20th, at Balaclava on October 25th, and at Inkerman on November 5th. After a year-long siege, the Russian naval base at Sevastopol surrendered to the allies on September 10th, 1855. The new Russian Tsar, Alexander II, signed a surrender in Paris on March 30th, 1856. This ended the war and secured the neutrality of the Black Sea.

## CHARGE OF THE LIGHT BRIGADE

The Charge of the Light Brigade (below) at Balaclava was one of Britain's most notorious military actions. As a result of confusion over some orders, a brigade of light cavalry were ordered to charge down a narrow valley 1.5 miles long, straight at thirty Russian cannon with batteries on either side. One of the cavalry regiments was the 17th Lancers (below).

*A bugle used in the charge of the Light Brigade*

## HOSPITALS

The medical conditions for men who were injured in battle were appalling. After reports of the terrible sanitation in a hospital in Scutari, Turkey, appeared in the newspapers, a woman called Florence

Nightingale (left) obtained permission to take nurses to the Crimea to clean up the hospital. When she arrived on November 7th, 1854, doctors refused to help her until they became overloaded with wounded men from the Battle of Inkerman. At that time, up to 42 percent of admitted casualties died in the rat-infested hospital. With Nightingale's strict regime of cleanliness and the nurses' efforts, this was cut to 2 percent.

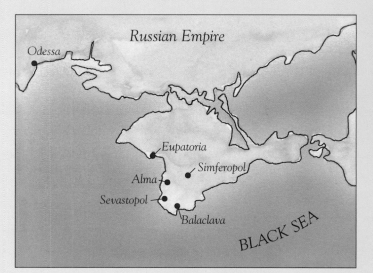

*Map showing the major battles of the Crimean War (above)*

Shako helmet

Lance

Blue double-breasted uniform

Cartridge box

## A MASSACRE

Out of the 607 brigadiers who rode out in the Charge of the Light Brigade, only 198 returned. Although the brave and risky charge had no military value, the British won the battle against a much stronger Russian force.

*Recreation of a member of the Light Brigade*

America

# AMERICAN CIVIL WAR

From 1861 to 1865, America was torn apart by a civil war between northern (Union) and southern (Confederate) states. The conflict arose over laws imposed on the southern states by the national government, headed by President Lincoln. Some individual states wanted to govern themselves. Thirty years of quarrels over issues including trade and slavery, finally erupted into war. It was the first major conflict to make use of 19th-century technology. Generals communicated with each other by telegraph, balloons were used to spy on enemy positions, ironclad ships started to replace wooden ships, and troops and supplies were moved by trains.

In the late stages of the war, trench warfare developed. Barbed wire and early machine guns were used on the battlefield. Around 600,000 people died, making it the bloodiest war in the history of America. It could be said the Civil War was the first "modern" war and an indicator of the carnage to come in World War I.

Bayonet scabbard

Musket

Recreation of a soldier in the Union army

A UNION SOLDIER
For the wealthier Union army, uniforms were standard—a dark blue jacket and sky-blue pants. Equipment included a knapsack, a rolled blanket, a cartridge box, a water-bottle, and a rifle fixed with a bayonet. Muskets now had spiral grooves, or rifling, which made a musket ball spin. This gave the weapon a longer range and better accuracy.

Map showing America on the eve of the Civil War

Union states

Confederate states

States which later joined the Confederacy

The southern Confederate states were Alabama, Mississippi, Arkansas, Georgia, Tennessee, Virginia, Texas, Louisiana, Florida, and North and South Carolina. Nebraska and Kansas were bought from France in the 1803 Louisiana Purchase. In 1836, Texas won its independence from Mexico and became a state in 1845. California and New Mexico were gained in the Mexican War of 1848.

*A pistol with attached bayonet for close combat*

### PISTOLS
At the beginning of the war, neither army had an official pistol, but by the end, pistols were being manufactured in the thousands.

### REPEATING RIFLES
The Spencer carbine was issued to Union troops as a cavalry firearm in late 1863. The gun was both superbly crafted and highly accurate. With its seven-round capacity, it proved to be a very effective weapon for firing on horseback. It was nicknamed "Spencer and his seven devils."

### A CONFEDERATE SOLDIER
The poorer Confederate army had little means of manufacturing clothing. They wore gray and brown makeshift uniforms (right). In the later stages of the war, they often used parts of captured Union soldiers' uniforms and weapons. A Confederate carried a knapsack, a cartridge box, a wooden water-bottle, and a rifle with a bayonet. Across his shoulder was a blanket roll. He often kept a tin pot for making coffee. Infantrymen used long muskets, but cavalry units on both sides favored the shorter carbine.

Blanket roll

Water-bottle

Bayonet

Musket

*Recreation of a soldier in the Confederate army*

*Butt of a Spencer carbine rifle*

# THE UNION VICTORY

ULYSSES S. GRANT
Grant (1822–1885), seated third from left in the photo above, entered the war as a colonel of volunteers in support of the Union and was rapidly promoted. He was later President of the U.S. from 1867 to 1877.

The first major battle of the American Civil War proved that there would be no easy victory for the Union troops. They were driven back when they tried to break through Confederate lines at Bull Run, Virginia. Later in the war, their superior numbers and better equipment set them ahead. The Confederates repeatedly attempted to rally and fight back, but they spent a great deal of time in retreat. In the Battle of Gettysburg in July 1863, they suffered overwhelming casualties. The Confederate commander, General Lee, was forced to surrender his last 7,800 troops on April 9th, 1865, at Appomattox in Virginia.

## ARTILLERY
The war saw a progressive transition from smooth-bore to rifled field guns by both sides.

## GUNSHIPS
Floating mortar vessels had no engines but could heavily bombard enemy positions on land.

## TRAINS
The Union used trains to move men, supplies, and artillery to needed locations. This gave them an advantage.

## IRONCLADS
These new, heavily-armored warships were almost indestructible. When the *Merrimac* (Confederate) and the *Monitor* (Union) met in battle on March 9th, 1862, the battle raged for four hours before being called off, because the men were exhausted from loading the cannon.

*The Union army attacking at Gettysburg*

## ROBERT E. LEE
Lee (1807–1870, left) was the leading Confederate general. He became the military advisor to the President of the Southern Confederacy, Jefferson Davis. In 1862, he commanded the Northern Army in victories at Fredericksburg and Chancellorsville. He was a great commander and sometimes defeated larger Union armies with his superior tactics.

# AMERICAN INDIAN WARS, 1854–90

*A colt revolver as used in the "Wild West"*

In the mid 1800s, a great stream of pioneers, ranchers, and gold panners poured into the "Wild West." They brought with them diseases like smallpox, which wiped out whole tribes of Native Americans. White hunters slaughtered millions of buffalo, and farmers fenced off the huge open plains. One by one, the tribes were forced off their land and onto reservations by the U.S. government. Most went peacefully, but others chose to fight. The most famous victory was at the Battle of the Little Big Horn. But the Native American tribes could never entirely defeat the larger and more powerful U.S. army. The soldiers burnt their villages and showed no mercy. By 1890, no Plains Indians remained free.

GENERAL GEORGE CUSTER
Called "Long Hair" by the Native Americans, Custer (above) was in command of the 7th Cavalry. He had served in the Civil War on the Union side. He attacked Chief Sitting Bull's huge camp at the Little Big Horn in 1876, but Custer's men were defeated and all 265 men were killed.

*General*

*Captain*

*Cavalryman*   *Native American scout*

INSIDE A FORT
Each captain was in charge of a company of 25 men. A sergeant kept discipline and gave day-to-day orders. Senior officers, such as generals and colonels, would visit the fort to pass on government orders, negotiate treaties with the Indians, or organize attacks against them. Cavalrymen carried sabers, revolvers, and rifles. Native American scouts were used to find camps or guide soldiers along trails.

FORT LARAMIE
Fort Laramie (right), Wyoming, was a post thriving with trappers, miners, Native Americans, and pioneers on their way westwards. Later, during the Indian Wars, the U.S. army built forts all over the West, and Fort Laramie became a military complex.

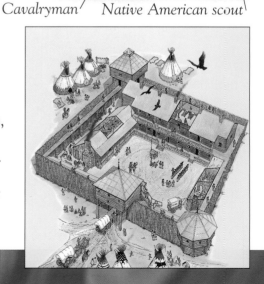

Recreation of a
Native American fighter

War paint

Bone
breastplate

Rifle and case

Native American warriors, like this Cheyenne
(left), fought on horseback. They wore war paint to
make themselves look fierce. Their weapons' cases
for guns and bows had decorative bead work, as did
their moccasins. They wore a breastplate made out
of bone and carried a shield to protect themselves.

Bow

Shield

SITTING BULL
A warrior and medicine man,
Sitting Bull was the most
famous of all the Sioux Indians.
Along with other chiefs,
he led his warriors in a war
against men who were trying to
drive Native Americans onto
reservations. After Little Big
Horn, he fled to Canada but
eventually surrendered.

NATIVE AMERICAN TACTICS
The tribes often used hit-and-run
tactics (below), avoiding open
battles where they would be
out-gunned. They often laid
ambushes, drawing soldiers into
a trap by using a small group of
warriors as bait.

Moccasins

Native American
rider's gauntlets

# TIME LINE

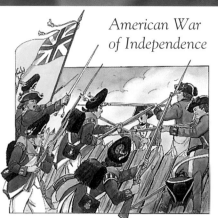

*American War of Independence*

## 1550–1650
Warring feudal nobles with samurai armies fight over territories in Japan.

## 1587
Francis Drake makes an expedition to Cadiz and destroys 33 Spanish ships.

*English warship*

## 1588
The Spanish Armada attacks England and is repelled by English ships.

## 1642–1646
The English Civil War. King Charles I is beheaded in 1649.

## 1652
Following the *Navigations Act* (1651), England and the Netherlands are at war over control of sea routes and regulation of colonial trade.

## 1658
At the Battle of the Dunes, an Anglo-French alliance defeats the Spanish army.

## 1688
The "Glorious Revolution" in Britain. King James II is overthrown, and William of Orange is crowned King of Britain. In 1690, at the Battle of the Boyne, James is defeated in Ireland by William III (formerly William of Orange).

## 1701–1714
The War of the Spanish Succession. In the Battle of Blenheim (1704), the British and Prince Eugene of Savoy destroy an Franco-Bavarian force. In 1708, they defeat the French at Oudenarde.

## 1701
The Kingdom of Prussia is established.

## 1707
Scotland is formally joined with England and Wales to form the United Kingdom.

## 1745
The Jacobite rebellion. "Bonnie Prince Charlie" enters a conflict with George I over the right to the British throne and is defeated at the Battle of Culloden (1746).

## 1756–1763
The Seven Years' War was fought between Russia, Austria, and France against the expansion of Prussian power. Frederick II of Prussia defeats the Austrians at Prague in 1757. At the Battle of Zorndorf (1758), Frederick wins and ends the Russian threat. He is defeated by a Austro-Russian force at Kunersdorf in 1759. In 1763, the Treaty of Hubertusburg ends the Seven Years' War, after Tsar Peter III of Russia begins peace talks.

## 1761–1762
The Spanish try to invade Portugal but are driven back.

## 1775–1783
The American War of Independence. The first shots are fired at Lexington. George Washington takes command of the Continental Army. After a siege, the British abandon Boston. France and Spain give support to the American side. The Battle of Bemis Heights, Saratoga, is an American victory and the turning point in the war. In 1781, the Americans besiege Yorktown, and British General Cornwallis surrenders.

## 1782
Britain signs the Treaty of Paris, recognizing U.S. independence.

## 1797–1815
The Napoleonic Wars. French Emperor Napoleon's Egyptian expedition defeats the Egyptian Mamelukes at Cairo, and the French fleet is almost destroyed by Nelson.

## 1800
Napoleon crosses the Alps into Italy.

## 1805
British Admiral Nelson wins at the Battle of Trafalgar but loses

*Battle of Trafalgar*

his life to a French sniper. Napoleon wins battles at Ulm and Austerlitz.

### 1806
Napoleon wins at Jena, enters Berlin, and carries on to Warsaw.

### 1808
Napoleon starts his Spanish campaign.

### 1809
The French win the Battle of Wagram against the Austrians.

### 1812–1813
Napoleon attacks Russia and marches to Moscow to find the city in flames. He retreats and his army lose more than 300,000 men in the winter conditions.

### 1814
While Napoleon resists invasion by Russia, Austria, and Prussia, the British Duke of Wellington advances into France from Spain and takes Toulouse. Meanwhile, Paris is taken by the eastern allies. Napoleon goes into exile on the island of Elba.

*Napoleon Bonaparte*

### 1815
Napoleon escapes from Elba and returns to France. He meets Wellington's army at Waterloo and is defeated after the late arrival of the Prussians.

### 1854–1856
The Crimean War. French, British, and Ottoman Turks fight against the Russians' invasion of the Turkish-controlled Christian holy land.

### 1854
Allied forces defeat the Russians at Alma, Balaclava, and Inkerman.

### 1855
France and Britain capture Sevastopol after a yearlong siege.

### 1856
Peace treaty signed at Paris ends the Crimean War.

### 1861
The American Civil War begins. Southerners shell Union-held Fort Sumter in South Carolina. Union forces advance on the southern capital, Richmond.

### 1863
Confederate General Lee loses the Battle at Gettysburg with 31,000 casualties.

### 1864
Union General Grant invades the South with a larger and better equipped army. Lee's Northern Army is pinned down defending Petersburg and Richmond.

### 1865
On April 9th, General Lee is forced to surrender at Appomattox, Virginia, ending the war. On April 14th, President Lincoln is assassinated.

### 1854
The American Indian Wars begin.

### 1862
Little Crow the Younger leads a Sioux uprising.

### 1870
The Franco-Prussian War lasts 44 days. Napoleon III of France surrenders on September 2nd at Sedan to Kaiser William.

### 1874
Colonel Mackenzie defeats the Comanches at Red River.

### 1876
Chief Sitting Bull unifies the Sioux and defeats General Custer at the Battle of the Little Big Horn.

*American Indian Wars*

### 1877
The famous Native warrior Crazy Horse is killed at Fort Robinson, Nebraska.

### 1889
Geronimo surrenders.

### 1890
The Battle of Wounded Knee. The final battle of the American Indian Wars occurs.

# GLOSSARY

**Armada**  A large number of ships.

**Artillery**  High caliber guns.

**Bandolier**  A soldier's shoulder belt with small pockets or loops for gun cartridges.

**Battery**  An artillery unit.

**Bayonet**  A blade attached to a gun used for close combat fighting.

**Cache**  A store of weapons.

**Cartridges**  Ammunition for firearms.

**Casualty**  A soldier killed or wounded in enemy action.

**Cavalier**  A supporter of King Charles I during the English Civil War.

**Cavalry**  Troops who fight on horseback.

**Clan**  A group of families with a common ancestor.

**Colony**  A territory occupied and ruled by a foreign state.

**Confederacy**  The southern states which fought the Union in the American Civil War.

**Continental**  The name given to the British who fought to keep the 13 northern states in the American Revolution.

**Drill**  Military training.

**Empire**  Territory under the rule of a sovereign state.

**Exile**  A forced absence from one's home or country.

**Expansionism**  The policy of expanding the territory of a country.

**Gold panner**  Someone searching for gold.

**Grenade**  An explosive thrown by hand.

**Infantry**  Soldiers who fight on foot.

**Ironclad**  A warship with iron plating.

**Jacobite**  A Scottish follower of James II.

**Mocassins**  Soft leather shoes.

**Morale**  The spirit of optimism within a group or individual.

**Ottoman Empire**  The Turkish empire.

**Privateer**  A privately owned ship authorized by government.

**Redcoat**  A type of British soldier.

**Reservation**  An area of land set aside for American Indians.

**Revolver**  A pistol with a cylindrical chamber.

**Roundhead**  A supporter of Parliament during the English Civil War.

**Royalist**  A supporter of the ruling monarch.

**Saber**  A type of sword with a curved blade.

**Samurai**  A Japanese warrior.

**Shogun**  A Japanese military commander.

**Smallpox**  A highly contagious disease.

**Sniper**  A concealed rifleman.

**Speaking trumpet**  An instrument that makes the speaker's voice louder.

**Succession**  When the leadership of a nation passes from one person to another.

**Tactics**  Military maneuvers to outwit an enemy.

**Taxes**  A compulsory payment issued to the government.

**Treaty**  An agreement between nations or states.

**Uniform**  Clothing that identifies which side of a battle a soldier belongs to.

**Union**  The northern states in the American Civil War.

**Volunteer**  A person who serves their country willingly.

# INDEX

Page numbers in **bold** refer to illustrations.